WHISKEY,
WORDS, AND A
SHOVEL

BY

R. H. SIN

UNDERWATER MOUNTAINS PUBLISHING
LOS ANGELES, CALIFORNIA
A SECRET COMPANY.

WHISKEY, WORDS, AND A SHOVEL
WRITTEN BY R. H. SIN
EDITED AND ARRANGED BY
WILLIAM MATHEW PEASTER & ASHLEY GAINES

To the woman I love : Samantha King

Thank you for your patience and understanding. I met you in a time where my heart was completely cracked, my soul visibly dark and my mind was nearly lost. You've filled me up with so much peace and love. I want you to know as well as the rest of the world, that I love you and I am forever grateful for your presence. I've spent years searching for a love like yours and for a moment, someone like you only existed in my dreams but then I met you. You are of great value, a Queen. Thanks for making me feel like a King. You are proof that heaven is attainable without death. You are proof of prayers coming true.

To my best friend: Aysha Norman

Thank you for encouraging me to keep writing. We've been friends for over 15 years and you believed that this book would happen for so long. The many years where I'd share this plan to one day express my thoughts to the world and you listened to my crazy ideas without judging me. Your friendship has definitely made as impact on my life and art. May you shine like the star you've always been.

To my Mother, my first love: Dahlia Holmes

Thank you for bringing me into this world and teaching me all that I know. Thank you for teaching me discipline, self respect and self love. These words, my enlightenment comes from your teachings and you will forever be immortalized within every word of wisdom I spill upon these pages. You will forever be immortalized within the sweet, painful, witty and beautiful things I express to the world.

WHISKEY,
WORDS, AND A
SHOVEL

BY

R. H. SIN

(whiskey wordplay)

A lot of men fear the waves of
your ocean, so much they'd
prefer puddles and that's fine.

(1 a.m. restless)

Memories are silent killers
the way they creep up unannounced
disguising themselves as innocent
knowing damn well
they intend to do harm
and if that's the case
tonight, you'll be the death of me.

(conversations with self under moonlight)

I remember laying there, quiet.
Fading into the silence of four
walls and a window that
allowed the moon to stare at
me. Thinking to myself, "you
can't force someone to realize
that you're what's best for
them."

(the illusion of a good morning)

She was his morning coffee
enough to keep him awake
until he found someone else
to use to his advantage.

(misplaced energy)

Loving you was draining.
Instead of wasting
my emotional energy, I decided
to forgive you and move on.

(something for the night)

Tonight won't be easy
and you know that
I know it hurts
but the pain is necessary
everything meant to tear you down
will build you up
and make you stronger.

(broken beautiful muse)

Broken, I cut myself trying to help her put it back together. Her heart was in pieces, on the bathroom floor. The door was closed and I could hear her weeping even as I was sleeping. Curious to the sound, awoken by her efforts to hide what she could no longer keep hidden. Broken, yet as I looked into her ocean filled eyes, I saw strength. We were different people after that night. She'd go on knowing that at least one person cared and I went on, using a woman's strength as my muse. Broken she was and still she inspired something so beautiful.

(forward, beyond the past)

Come,
I'll help you
bury your past
we'll give life
to our future.

(past and present)

I'm always moving on
you're always coming back
you only reappear
when you fear you've been replaced
the never ending cycle of what we were
yet you'll forever be nothing more
than a constant mistake.

(cold)

It was your love that caused
this. It was you that made me
this way. Suddenly being
heartless was better than being
heart broken. Being cold was
better than the warmth you
failed to provide.

(all of the people)

All these people with pain in
their faces, bruises on their
souls, and cracks in their hearts.
We're all trying to survive the
death of what we thought was
love. We're all just trying to
make sense of a reality that is
now a lie.

(easier said than done)

And sometimes I wish changing
my heart was as easy as
changing my mind.

(a good heart)

The only downfall of having a
good heart is that you're
constantly looking for angels
inside of demons. And they
wonder why the good know so
much pain.

(devour)

Devour her the right way and
her back will rise off the bed,
she'll bite her lip, and her
thighs will begin to tremble.
Devour her the right way and
she'll begin to flood the
surface of your lips.

(heart vs. mind)

The heart takes too long
to figure out what the mind
already knows. I hate that.

(peacefulness)

First I missed you then I
learned to live without
you. I found comfort in
your absence, I made
peace with being alone.

(midnight memories)

Midnight belonged to us
she was always down
and I was always up.

(restless)

Stop losing sleep over someone
who can't even find time to
consider you. Take your ass to
sleep, he doesn't deserve your
thoughts tonight.

(thinking out loud)

I set fire to every memory
we made then smiled
as I watched us go up in flames.

(the last resort)

There's something sad about the fact
that he only reaches out to you
late into the evening
secretly admitting
that he could care less about
you during daylight,
horny & bored
he chooses to pursue you under the moon.

(wanting)

I guess what we want is
someone who only wants us.
Sounds simple doesn't it? Yet
some set out to find this and
die trying. Not the death
which means the ending of life
in the literal sense but the
burial of one's heart as they
decide that love isn't for them.

(your essence)

Baby
you're a star
don't apologize
for burning too bright.

(Ocean Marie)

With two fingers
and a few strokes
she began to over flow
and I was ready to drown.

(fighting temptation)

She knew I was taken
she knew I was in love
she offered up herself
but I declined
see, pussy can only sway
a weak man and cause him to stray
my love for my lover is so much stronger
than anything anyone else could ever offer.

(do more)

She's not easily impressed.
Those shallow compliments
mean nothing. She needs more.
She deserves me.

(2:28 a.m.)

Heart break changed the temperature of my heart
your lies became bricks which I used
to build this wall
the barrier that sheltered and kept my love safe
also kept new love from getting in.

(whiskey fights)

I yelled because I care. I argue because I give a fuck. One day I'll be silent, and that's when your ass should begin to worry.

(consistency)

I asked for consistency and
you consistently destroyed
the best parts of me. I guess
I should have been a bit
clearer with what I was asking
for.

(alone)

No one wants to be alone
but no one wants to feel the loneliness
of being with the wrong person.

(brave)

She wore her scars
on the inside
and you'd never know
her pain
as she chooses not
to complain
so much strength in a woman.

(angels and demons)

You're an angel, stop letting
these devils undress you.

(every night)

Every night, the same old shit.
You wait up for a call that never
comes while he misses out on
the opportunity to hear your
voice. I know its hard feeling
the way you do. I know you're
tired of the restlessness you
experience, laying down while
reading this book but just
remember these next few lines.
You are strong, intelligent,
worth it, and beautiful. You
deserve so much more than
you've chosen to accept.

(early july)

They say the tongue gives life,
so I spoke into her.

(fire within)

There are flames in my soul,
deep where no water can reach
me and as I continue to burn,
I enjoy the smell. Even though it
hurts like hell.

(pieces of peace)

Amazing isn't it
the way your broken pieces
give me peace
you've been broken
and yet
you're still able
to make me feel whole.

(searching for love)

Angels going through hell
in search of love, dating
demons.

(temporary)

You were only meant to be
temporary. I wish I knew that
before I spoke you into my
future.

(a slow death)

Slowly death crept up behind me
and as my grip got tighter
holding onto you
was killing me.

(book of ashes)

Together we wrote the book on
our relationship, tonight I'll
burn the pages.

(deserving of more)

You always end up trying to
please someone who isn't even
satisfied with themselves.
You're constantly searching for
a love within someone who
doesn't even value themselves.
You've been wasting your time,
holding onto someone who
doesn't even care about
keeping you.

(great wall)

Maybe she built that wall in
front of her heart in order to
save herself from the pain she's
become familiar with. Maybe
she's protecting her heart from
anyone not willing to climb that
wall and claim the love which
she refuses to give away so
easily.

(into chaos)

I followed my heart. It led me
straight into chaos. I nearly lost
my damn mind.

(lines)

There's just something about her
the type of high my mind craves
she's the feeling of late nights
after hours on Fridays
she's my good-time girl
when stressed out
she helps me cope
like an actor doing lines
she's always been my coke.

(on the inside)

Her tears are rarely visible
the sound of silence
as she screams on the inside
scars and bruises
in places you'll never see
overthinking
filled with words
she'll never speak
going through hell
she'll never tell
she has a guard up
refusing to believe
the bull shit stories
of which they tell.

(nothing forced)

I can't make you be faithful,
loyal and honest. I can't make
you appreciate everything that I
am but I can force you to live
without me as I invest my time
in someone better than you.

(life lesson)

I learned that someone who is
yours can never be taken away
and if for any reason you lose
your lover to someone else,
that person never deserved to
be claimed by you.

(moonlit)

She's the moon
just laying there alone
she shines in darkness.

(right now)

Somewhere, right now
someone is searching for everything
that you have
everything that you once thought
wasn't good enough
beautiful the way it works
what was once treated with hate
will one day be loved
by the one deserving of you.

(vanish)

I became a ghost to
you. You missed me,
sometimes you felt me
but you could no longer
see me. I've learned to
vanish from those who
fail to appreciate my
presence.

(whiskey with dinner)

The truth was no longer on the menu and love was no longer being served. That's why I left the table. I'd rather eat alone.

(the little things)

If you don't love the way
her eyes squint when she smiles
or the way her lips curl when she laughs
stop wasting her fucking time.

(still beautiful)

You're not perfect. There are scars on the surface of your heart. I'm convinced that you've experienced a set of painful events throughout your life and you are what people refer to as broken. In my eyes, you're the most beautiful arrangement of broken I've ever witnessed. I look at you and think, "there's my future, she's the one."

(the path)
Some paths lead to a lifetime of loneliness
it is our choices in things and people that often
shape our future
so when you chose someone other than me
you destroyed what could have been
your happy ending
the one you chose will choose someone else
when faced with the same decision
and you'll essentially be alone.

(visibly strong)

She wore pain like it didn't
hurt, smiling through the
heartache and sorrow.

(sin.ergy)

Just like me
you're a sinner
and I'm your accomplice
on your knees
against the wall
on your back
I'm always there.

(reminder)

Just because you're broken doesn't
mean you're not beautiful and a moment
of weakness doesn't mean you're not
strong.

(perfect aim)

Willingly, I'll walk away
and I won't miss you
this .45 fits perfectly in my hand
and my aim is so much better.

(optimistic)

& it hurts like hell, every minute
of every day but it'll get better.
One day you'll realize that everything
meant to destroy you, only made you
stronger.

(masks)

There was something so special about you
in the beginning
you were rare but time revealed
the most honest parts of you
and it turns out
everything about you was a lie
you were like the others.

(not a loss)

I find comfort in knowing that
I've only lost those who didn't
deserve to stay.

(false claims of love)

You run around writing about a love that never existed. A love claimed by a man who only used the word to get what he was after. You called it a relationship when all he did was stick around just to sample what he'd never truly commit to. Taking what he could before he left. This is the reality of what you claim is love.

(apology)

I'm sorry for thinking
that you took us
seriously.

(before then after)

I'm just not who I was before you
I allowed you into a place
untouched by the hands of anyone
I held the door open
just so that you could walk in
and make a home out of me
you took my willingness to allow you close
and destroyed the insides of my heart
you took the trust that I gave unto you
and threw it away as if to say
"this is garbage"
before you, I was different
after you, i'll never be the same.

(constantly)

That's your problem
you're constantly
searching for paradise
where only hell exists

you're constantly
searching for peace
in a place where only
chaos lives

you've been
expecting love
from the same person
who treats you
with so much hate

hope kills
when invested
in the wrong people.

(flames)

She was the flame that no one
could put out. Burning brighter
than the sun, refusing to be
taken lightly. She was driven by
all the things that caused her
pain as what failed to weaken
her flames became fuel. She is
you.

(I wanted her)

Show me the woman with scars
in her mind from overthinking,
cracks in her heart from loving
the wrong person, and pain attached
to her soul, and I'll fight for
the chance to love
her.

(hostage)

He kidnapped your heart, held
your emotions hostage with no
intent to love you.

(reasons why)

& that's why we stay longer
than we should because it hurts
to watch something you love
transform into something you
hate. We sit & wait for it to
return to its original state,
in denial as we ignore the fact
that what we see was always
there & what is now, will always
be.

(limited)

We could have been great
but you insisted on being mediocre
you placed limitations on us
so I chose myself;
I deserved more.

(sin's theory)

You can't keep a man
who doesn't deserve you.
Maybe that's why they leave.

(word porn)

She wanted to be taken
mentally starved by a mind
incapable of stimulating hers
my knowledge and understanding
like food to a dying soul
I became the only thing
she could think about
rooftops, lying wide-awake
and vulnerable under the bright moon
in lust with the way I spoke
my open mind kept her open
every word was like a thrust
or stroke as she invited me
to spill my words on her canvas.

(she let go)

Maybe that's all she wanted, to be acknowledged.
To be appreciated for the things she did, someone
who cared enough to show it. A man who could love
her in the same fashion as she loved him. I don't think
she was asking for too much, all which she demanded
was simply what she deserved. You served her a bunch
of lies and expected her to get full, starving her of the
truth, but one day it happened. The woman which you
only wanted to break reached a point in which she
could break no longer, though you thought she'd
hold on longer. She let go.

(passive aggressive)

I'll say nothing
I'll be silent
you have my word
or lack thereof
but if you forget
to choose me
you'll lose me.

(she's an artist)

She was broken. Yes, but somehow she found peace in the pieces left behind. She's an artist in the way she pieces herself back together to form something stronger and a bit more beautiful than before.

(one of those days)

It's like sunshine
peeking through dark
clouds. I should be
happy but I'm not.

(lust in darkness)

It wasn't love
I was just obsessed with the way
you made me feel on satin sheets
under the moon.

(june)

What was meant to be a
celebration, now feels like a
funeral.

(in waiting)

I was more in love with who
I thought you were, and I hated
who you became. Hoping the
version of you who cared for
me would return.

(holding on)

Stop holding onto someone,
who is obviously reaching for
someone else.

(friends with benefits)

The fucked up thing
about using someone for sex
is that you're probably getting used
just the same
by someone who doesn't deserve
a portion of anything you have to share
you're using them while wasting yourself
you think you're winning
yet you're constantly losing.

(crown me)

She crowned the tip of my
head with the lips between
her thighs. My Queen made
me King.

(a sharp tongue)

Lies are like razors. You claimed
to be telling the truth yet
I watched you bleed from your
mouth.

(choices)

I didn't have the courage to
love you in the way you
needed. You wouldn't let go,
and so I let go for us, for you.

(after midnight)

After midnight is when we
often remember the things we
try our hardest to forget.

(early december)

She was the most beautiful type
of broken I'd ever seen in my
entire life and even though her
heart was in pieces, she
deserved to be loved.

(observation)

It's crazy how the women who
smile the most are often the
ones who experience the most
pain. She doesn't wear a smile
to deceive others. She smiles
because she's trying to remain
strong, trying to keep it together
though inside she feels like
she's falling apart.

(lie & pretend)

We all want someone to notice
our sadness and when they do,
we lie and pretend to be happy.

(maybe)

Maybe you're the strong one
maybe you hold on
because you're strong enough to love
unconditionally
and maybe they're just too weak
to appreciate it.

(wound)

You were broken
and I cut myself
trying to get close to you
I tried several times
I almost bled out for you.

(us, the future)

Come, I'll help you bury
your past. We'll give life
to our future.

(sober thoughts)

I've been missing you
either I'll run out of bullets
or improve my aim
that's where my mind is at
pushing forward into the future
lost count of how often
I took you back.

(the morning after)

And so it happens
you wake up one morning
and the feelings you went
to sleep with are no longer
there
you picture life without that person
and instead of feeling worried
you begin to smile.

(sin's request)

I want everything he took for granted.
I have this craving to explore the parts
of you he neglected, but first I'll work for it.
Everything within you is not to be given
but earned.

(repetitive)

Found pain,
searching for
love...

(i'm sorry)

We do that sometimes.
We ask you to give us
your all and when you do,
we leave.

(distant from self)

I've been losing me for a while
my reflection appears partial
as I often feel less than I've been
and further away from the person
I'd like to be.

(burning bridges)

I never miss what I walk away from
there is no regret in walking away
from someone who gave me a reason
to leave them behind
I'm the one who burns bridges
just to light my path to a new direction
I'm the one who uses failed friendships
and relationships as stepping stones.

(invisible)

Her scars weren't visible. She
was hurt in places no one could
actually see.

(I miss you texts)

I take "I miss you" with a grain of salt.
Those texts are always coming in at the
most random times and from people
who failed to cherish the time I invested
in them. They send these texts
in an attempt to get an emotional
response from me but I say nothing in
return. I don't have time for those who
only find time for me because they
failed to replace the irreplaceable while
searching for me in everyone they
meet.

(lustful and lust filled)

Our love was weak, only
exchanged over the strength of
a climax experienced in the
back seat of a vehicle or on the
floor next to the mattress we
rarely slept on.

(journal entry)

It's always been easy for me
to get someone into my bed
but finding that one person whom
deserved to lie next to me was
something I struggled with.

(painful truth)

And she pretended this was love
because the truth was too painful
and the loneliness was unbearable.

(short story)

He moved on
& she stayed there
waiting longer than she should have
he let go
yet she held onto nothing
afraid to be alone
even though loneliness was all she felt
while with him.

(no explanations)

I usually become a ghost to
those who no longer deserve
my time. I've never seen a point
in explaining my absence to
someone who failed to
appreciate my presence. You
don't owe any explanations to
those who hurt you.

(self-love)

One day your love for yourself
will outweigh the love
that keeps you holding onto someone
who chooses to hurt you;
one day the love for yourself
will be your strength—
that love will be more than enough reason
for you to walk away for good.

(the next)

I no longer grieve the ending of
any of my relationships because
I know what's next is better
than what I had and whatever
belongs to me, will remain with
me. I can't lose the one who
deserves to be a part of my life.

(soul restless)

It never gets easier
the late nights under the moon
restless, unable to retrieve sleep
slowly losing yourself
so far from who you were
yet unable to be who you should
it never gets easier
you just get stronger
even if you don't feel it.

(potential)

You were everything I should have avoided,
but your potential kept me in a place
of sadness, waiting for you to change;
but that day never came.

(loyalty)

Because that's how it's always been
the more loyal you are
the more familiar you become with betrayal
always giving the opposite of what you
receive from others.

(flat-line)

You're losing me, we're
losing us. We're so much
closer to flat-lining. Death is
becoming our future, a slow
death has become our path.

(hell for an angel)

In the name of love, an
angel goes through hell.

(emotionally closed)

I don't like to open up to people much. The more you do, the more they don't understand. The more frustrated you become, the worse you feel.

(conversation in july)

Because every guy "loved" you,
just not enough to stay.

(eventually)

One day
what you know
will overshadow
what you feel

on that day
your emotions
will no longer
corrupt your judgment

the love for yourself
will outweigh
what you've felt
for all the wrong people

this will be the day
in which
your heart
won't be able to
dictate your mind.

(tainted love)

Love isn't supposed to be
violent yet he claims it's love,
treating you as if he hates you.

(the one to change him)

She thought she'd be the one to change him. She thought holding on would prove her loyalty and commitment to things getting better, but she failed to realize that none of what she did made a difference or mattered to someone who wasn't emotionally available to acknowledge it.

(second chances)

You're always taking them back. You're always providing second chances. You know damn well if you fucked up just as much as them, they wouldn't do the same for you.

(what hurts)

All of a sudden you're the one texting first
and even then those conversations are cut
short by one word replies and or a delayed response.
Things are different now. While they're letting go,
you still want to try and that's what hurts.

(the death of us)

6 feet under
the greatest way to dispose of us
it was hard at first
the memories of who you were
often clouded my judgement
emotionally, blurring my visibility,
lost in a haze of confusion
realizing that what appeared to be love
was just an effort made by you
to manipulate my emotions for your own purpose
destroying my every means of contact
with those who truly cared for me
forced to abandon them
by the guilt trips you caused
choosing you would eventually mean
choosing death
and so tonight, I bury us.

(emotional truth)

Fuck you for making me feel
all the things you refused to. I
fell for your lies and landed
here on a pile of my own
truth. I was in love with the
idea of us but not in love with
you.

(december 10th)

Let me see the things you hid
from everyone else
strip away all of your barriers
feed me your essence
feed your soul
feed me your truth.

(in the fire)

Who knew being with you
was simply a personal
invitation to hell.

(made to feel)

Made to feel unlovable by those who claimed to love me yet left me to fight alone. Made to feel like nothing because my best has never been good enough. This has become my truth and sometimes an awful excuse to hurt myself, to hurt them, to hurt you.

(she was you)

She was a woman
with a good heart
she fell victim
to a good liar.

(surviving us)

They say holding onto the
wrong person is a slow death
and I guess I was just trying to
survive you.

(returned to absence)

You can choose them over me
you can invest your time elsewhere
you can entertain those who will
never estimate to who I am
you can go & do all of those things
I won't be here when you return
vacant will be the place
in which you left me
and there won't be anything
for you to come back to.

(still an angel)

You may have danced with
the devil unintentionally once
or twice but that doesn't mean
you don't deserve something
heavenly.

(rehab)

You used to be my favorite
drug, but you no longer get me
high.

(preference)

You've always been gold
but some men prefer
anything less than silver
and that's fine
you're not meant
for just anyone and everyone.

(my emptiness)

I was always trying to fill the empty
spaces in my heart with the sight of you
on your knees & the softness of your lips.

(symbols of survival)

These cracks in my heart don't just represent pain. They're symbols of how often I survived heartache and everything set in my path with the intent to destroy me.

(pain)

Sometimes the things we do to numb the pain, cause more pain.

(silent screams)

People rarely listen
you speak calmly
and a respectful tone gets you ignored
yet you say it loudly
and this seems to always complicate things
making all that you've decided to express
difficult to comprehend
that's why you choose to say nothing
thinking you'll be heard
just as long as you scream in silence
maybe then, they'll understand.

(revenge)

And then I used the broken
pieces of my heart to cut you
even deeper than you cut me.

(self-betrayal)

I betrayed my own
body, sleeping with
you. I betrayed my own
peace, while giving you
pieces of me.

(cheating death)

She was everything, made to
feel as if she wasn't enough.
Broken then beaten down by
her will to hold on to someone
who failed to keep the promises
made. She was hurt yet she
found a way to get through. She
survived the death of a
relationship that was no longer
worthy of her time.

(PSA: being single)

I think it's important for you to know
that it's okay to be single
and there is nothing wrong
with being by yourself for a while
do what makes you happy
even if it means walking away
from someone who failed to act on their
own potential
destroy the cycle of going back to things
that only provide you with reasons to walk away
you can't pursue happiness investing your time
in someone who would rather see you
miserable.

(she'll be fine)

There's a war inside her mind and bruises on her heart. She's just good at hiding it all from plain view. She got better at hiding what she didn't want the world to witness. Eyes swelling up with tears right now as she reads this. She'll be fine, she is you.

(the difference)

What she was to you is far more different
than who she is with me;
as you complained, I rejoice.
See, we won't have the same stories
about the same woman
because you failed at succeeding
in what I've done for her, easily.

(sober thoughts 2)

I think you're amazing
I think you've always been amazing
single or not
your relationship status
doesn't define your value
and being alone
doesn't determine your worth
being cheated on
doesn't mean you're not good enough
and the fact that you're hurting
doesn't mean that you're weak.

(similar)

You're just like me,
a broken shred of art,
and I want to love all of
your pieces.

WHISKEY, WORDS, AND A SHOVEL

A poetry book

by

R.H. Sin

INSTAGRAM: @R.H.SIN

A PRIVATE COMPANY

Elias Joseph Mennealy
Ryan Christopher Lutfalah
Christopher Poindexter

CPSIA information can be obtained at www.ICGtesting.com
Printed in the USA
BVOW08s2151080716

454608BV00002B/13/P